THE BEST OF
BRITISH COMEDY

LAST OF THE
SUMMER WINE

THE BEST OF
BRITISH COMEDY

LAST OF THE
SUMMER WINE

THE BEST SCENES, JOKES AND ONE-LINERS

Richard Webber

HarperCollins*Publishers*

HarperCollins*Publishers*
77–85 Fulham Palace Road,
Hammersmith, London W6 8JB
www.harpercollins.co.uk

First published by HarperCollins*Publishers* 2009

1

Scripts © Roy Clarke 2009
© Richard Webber Ltd 2009

The Author asserts the moral right to
be identified as the author of this work

A catalogue record of this book
is available from the British Library

ISBN 978-0-00-731897-1

Printed and bound in China
by Leo Paper Products Ltd

Picture credits: © Radio Times pp. 13, 19;
© Alan J W Bell pp. 25, 42, 58, 60, 75 (left), 98, 112,
117, 125, 129; © Malcolm Howarth pp. xxvi, 9, 16, 41,
49, 54, 75 (right), 78, 82, 93, 102, 106, 119.

ACKNOWLEDGEMENTS

This book wouldn't have been possible without Roy Clarke, who gave up valuable time to be interviewed and kindly allowed me to write about his fine sitcom and publish extracts from his many scripts. Thank you, Roy.

I'm also indebted to three walking *Summer Wine* encyclopaedias, namely Clive Eardley, Margaret Tillotson and Robert Hatton, all leading lights in the Last of the Summer Wine Appreciation Society. They have been fundamental in making this book possible, using their extensive knowledge of the sitcom to select some of the best scenes to publish in the book. Thanks for your invaluable help, especially when working to an extremely tight deadline and realising from the outset that choosing favourite scenes from over 280 shows would be excruciatingly difficult.

Then there is Alan J W Bell, the long-serving producer/director of *Summer Wine*. Not only did he give up a lot of time to discuss the show but he kindly allowed me to use many of his own photographs in the book. Other photos, meanwhile, were supplied by experienced photographer Malcolm Howarth, so thank you both.

Of course, there are many other people who have generously given up time to be interviewed or to help in a host of ways, such as Jimmy Gilbert and the actors – I'm indebted to you all. Last, but by no means least, thank you to my agent, Jeffrey Simmons and everyone at HarperCollins.

Finally, for further information about the Appreciation Society, formed in 1993, write to 18 Fairfield Avenue, Altofts, West Yorkshire WF6 2NH or ring 01924 893340.

EPISODE LIST

PILOT

'Of Funerals And Fish' (Transmitted 4/1/73)

SERIES 1

1. 'Short Back And Palais Glide' (12/11/73)
2. 'Inventor Of The Forty Foot Ferret' (19/11/73)
3. 'Pâté And Chips' (26/11/73)
4. 'Spring Fever' (3/12/73)
5. 'The New Mobile Trio' (10/12/73)
6. 'Hail Smiling Morn Or Thereabouts' (17/12/73)

SERIES 2

1. 'Forked Lightning' (5/3/75)
2. 'Who's That Dancing With Nora Batty, Then?' (12/3/75)

3. 'The Changing Face Of Rural Blamire' (19/3/75)
4. 'Some Enchanted Evening' (26/3/75)
5. 'A Quiet Drink' (2/4/75)
6. 'Ballad For Wind Instruments And Canoe' (9/4/75)
7. 'Northern Flying Circus' (16/4/75)

SERIES 3

1. 'The Man From Oswestry' (27/10/76)
2. 'Mending Stuart's Leg' (3/11/76)
3. 'The Great Boarding-House Bathroom Caper' (10/11/76)
4. 'Cheering Up Gordon' (17/11/76)
5. 'The Kink In Foggy's Niblick' (24/11/76)
6. 'Going To Gordon's Wedding' (1/12/76)
7. 'Isometrics And After' (8/12/76)

SERIES 4

1. 'Ferret Come Home' (9/11/77)
2. 'Getting On Sidney's Wire' (16/11/77)
3. 'Jubilee' (23/11/77)
4. 'Flower Power Cut' (30/11/77)
5. 'Who Made A Bit Of A Splash In Wales, Then?' (7/12/77)

6. 'Greenfingers' (21/12/77)

7. 'A Merry Heatwave' (1/1/78)

8. 'The Bandit From Stoke-On-Trent' (4/1/78)

CHRISTMAS SPECIAL

'Small Tune On A Penny Wassail' (26/12/78)

SERIES 5

1. 'Full Steam Behind' (18/9/79)

2. 'The Flag And Its Snags' (25/9/79)

3. 'The Flag And Further Snags' (2/10/79)

4. 'Deep In The Heart Of Yorkshire' (9/10/79)

5. 'Earnshaw Strikes Again' (16/10/79)

6. 'Here We Go Into The Wild Blue Yonder' (23/10/79)

7. 'Here We Go Again Into The Wild Blue Yonder' (30/10/79)

8. 'And A Dewhurst Up A Fir Tree' (27/12/79)

SERIES 6

1. 'Whoops' (25/12/81)

2. 'In The Service Of Humanity' (4/1/82)

3. 'Car And Garter' (11/1/82)

4. 'The Odd Dog Men' (18/1/82)

5. 'A Bicycle Made For Three' (25/1/82)

6. 'One Of The Last Few Places Unexplored By Man' (1/2/82)

7. 'Serenade For Tight Jeans And Metal Detector' (8/2/82)

8. 'From Wellies To Wet Suit' (15/2/82)

SERIES 7

1. 'All Mod Conned' (25/12/82)
2. 'The Frozen Turkey Man' (30/1/83)
3. 'The White Man's Grave' (6/2/83)
4. 'The Waist Land' (13/2/83)
5. 'Cheering Up Ludovic' (20/2/83)
6. 'The Three Astaires' (27/2/83)
7. 'The Arts Of Concealment' (6/3/83)

CHRISTMAS SPECIAL

'Getting Sam Home' (27/12/83)

CHRISTMAS SPECIAL

'The Loxley Lozenge' (30/12/84)

SERIES 8

1. 'The Mysterious Feet Of Nora Batty' (10/2/85)
2. 'Keeping Britain Tidy' (17/2/85)
3. 'Enter The Phantom' (24/2/85)
4. 'Catching Digby's Donkey' (3/3/85)
5. 'The Woollen Mills Of Your Mind' (10/3/85)
6. 'Who's Looking After The Café, Then?' (17/3/85)

CHRISTMAS SPECIAL

'Uncle Of The Bride' (1/1/86)

SERIES 9

1. 'Merry Christmas, Father Christmas' (28/12/86)
2. 'Why Does Norman Clegg Buy Ladies' Elastic Stockings?' (4/1/87)
3. 'The Heavily Reinforced Bottom' (11/1/87)
4. 'Dried Dates And Codfanglers' (18/1/87)
5. 'The Really Masculine Purse' (25/1/87)
6. 'Who's Feeling Ejected, Then?' (1/2/87)
7. 'The Ice-Cream Man Cometh' (8/2/87)
8. 'Set The People Free' (15/2/87)
9. 'Go With The Flow' (22/2/87)

10. 'Jaws' (1/3/87)
11. 'Edie And The Automobile' (8/3/87)
12. 'Wind Power' (15/3/87)
13. 'When You Take A Good Bite, Yorkshire Tastes Terrible' (22/3/87)

CHRISTMAS SPECIAL

'Big Day At Dream Acres' (27/12/87)

SERIES 10

1. 'The Experiment' (16/10/88)
2. 'The Treasure Of The Deep' (23/10/88)
3. 'Dancing Feet' (30/10/88)
4. 'That Certain Smile' (6/11/88)
5. 'Downhill Racer' (13/11/88)
6. 'The Day Of The Welsh Ferret' (20/11/88)

CHRISTMAS SPECIAL

'Crums' (24/12/88)

SERIES 11

1. 'Come Back Jack Harry Teesdale' (15/10/89)
2. 'The Kiss And Mavis Poskit' (22/10/89)
3. 'Oh Shut Up And Eat Your Choc Ice' (29/10/89)
4. 'Who's That Bloke With Nora Batty, Then?' (5/11/89)
5. 'Happy Anniversary, Gough And Jessie' (12/11/89)
6. 'Getting Barry Higher In The World' (19/11/89)
7. 'Three Men And A Mangle' (26/11/89)

CHRISTMAS SPECIAL

'What's Santa Brought For Nora, Then?' (23/12/89)

SERIES 12

1. 'Return Of The Warrior' (2/9/90)
2. 'Come In, Sunray Major' (9/9/90)
3. 'The Charity Balls' (16/9/90)
4. 'Walking Stiff Can Make You Famous' (23/9/90)
5. 'That's Not Captain Zero' (30/9/90)
6. 'Das (Welly) Boot' (7/10/90)
7. 'The Empire That Foggy Nearly Built' (14/10/90)
8. 'The Last Surviving Maurice Chevalier Impression' (21/10/90)

9. 'Roll On' (28/10/90)

10. 'A Landlady For Smiler' (4/11/90)

CHRISTMAS SPECIAL

'Barry's Christmas' (27/12/90)

SERIES 13

1. 'Quick, Quick, Slow' (18/10/91)
2. 'Give Us A Lift' (25/10/91)
3. 'Was That Nora Batty Singing?' (1/11/91)
4. 'Cashflow Problems' (8/11/91)
5. 'Passing The Earring' (15/11/91)
6. 'Pole Star' (29/11/91)

CHRISTMAS SPECIAL

'Situations Vacant' (22/12/91)

SERIES 14

1. 'By The Magnificent Thighs Of Ernie Burniston'
   (25/10/92)
2. 'Errol Flynn Used To Have A Pair Like That' (1/11/92)

3. 'The Phantom Of The Graveyard' (8/11/92)
4. 'The Self-Propelled Salad Strainer' (15/11/92)
5. 'Ordeal By Trousers' (22/11/92)
6. 'Happy Birthday, Howard' (29/11/92)
7. 'Who's Got Rhythm?' (6/12/92)
8. 'Camera Shy' (13/12/92)
9. 'Wheelies' (20/12/92)
10. 'Stop That Castle' (26/12/92)

SERIES 15

1. 'How To Clear Your Pipes' (24/10/93)
2. 'Where There's Smoke, There's Barbeque' (31/10/93)
3. 'The Black Widow' (7/11/93)
4. 'Have You Got A Light Mate?' (14/11/93)
5. 'Stop That Bath' (21/11/93)
6. 'Springing Smiler' (28/11/93)
7. 'Concerto For Solo Bicycle' (5/12/93)
8. 'There Are Gypsies At The Bottom Of Our Garden' (12/12/93)
9. 'Aladdin Gets On Your Wick' (19/12/93)
10. 'Welcome To Earth' (27/12/93)

SERIES 16

1. 'The Man Who Nearly Knew Pavarotti' (1/1/95)
2. 'The Glory Hole' (8/1/95)
3. 'Adopted By A Stray' (15/1/95)
4. 'The Defeat Of The Stoneworm' (22/1/95)
5. 'Once In A Moonlit Junkyard' (29/1/95)
6. 'The Space Ace' (5/2/95)
7. 'The Most Powerful Eyeballs In West Yorkshire' (12/2/95)
8. 'The Dewhirsts Of Ogleby Hall' (19/2/95)
9. 'The Sweet Smell Of Excess' (26/2/95)

SERIES 17

1. 'Leaving Home Forever Or Till Teatime' (3/9/95)
2. 'Bicycle Bonanza' (10/9/95)
3. 'The Glamour Of The Uniform' (17/9/95)
4. 'The First Human Being To Ride A Hill' (24/9/95)
5. 'Captain Clutterbuck's Treasure' (1/10/95)
6. 'Desperate For A Duffield' (8/10/95)
7. 'The Suit That Turned Left' (15/10/95)
8. 'Beware Of The Elbow' (22/10/95)
9. 'The Thing In Wesley's Shed' (29/10/95)
10. 'Brushes At Dawn' (5/11/95)

CHRISTMAS SPECIAL

'A Leg Up For Christmas' (24/12/95)

CHRISTMAS SPECIAL

'Extra! Extra!' (29/12/96)

SERIES 18

1. 'The Love Mobile' (20/4/97)
2. 'A Clean Sweep' (27/4/97)
3. 'The Mysterious C.W. Northrop' (4/5/97)
4. 'A Double For Howard' (11/5/97)
5. 'How To Create A Monster' (18/5/97)
6. 'Deviations With Davenport' (25/5/97)
7. 'According To The Prophet Bickerdyke' (1/6/97)
8. 'Next Kiss, Please' (8/6/97)
9. 'Destiny And Six Bananas' (15/6/97)
10. 'A Sidecar Named Desire' (22/6/97)

SERIES 19

1. 'There Goes The Groom' (29/12/97)
2. 'Beware Of The Oglethorpe' (4/1/98)

3. 'Tarzan Of The Towpath' (11/1/98)

4. 'Truly And The Hole Truth' (18/1/98)

5. 'Oh Howard, We Should Get One Of Those' (25/1/98)

6. 'The Suit That Attracts Blondes' (1/2/98)

7. 'The Only Diesel Saxophone In Captivity' (8/2/98)

8. 'Perfection – Thy Name Is Ridley' (15/2/98)

9. 'Nowhere Particular' (22/2/98)

10. 'From Audrey Nash To The Widow Dilhooley' (1/3/98)

11. 'Support Your Local Skydiver' (8/3/98)

SERIES 20

1. 'The Pony Set' (18/4/99)

2. 'How Errol Flynn Discovered The Secret Scar Of Nora Batty' (25/4/99)

3. 'Who's Thrown Her Tom Cruise Photographs Away?' (2/5/99)

4. 'What Happened To Barry's Nose?' (16/5/99)

5. 'Optimism In The Housing Market' (23/5/99)

6. 'Will Barry Go Septic Despite Listening To Classical Music?' (30/5/99)

7. 'Beware The Vanilla Slice' (6/6/99)

8. 'Howard Throws A Wobbler' (13/6/99)

9. 'The Phantom Number 14 Bus' (20/6/99)

10. 'Ironing Day' (27/6/99)

Millennium Special

'Last Post And Pigeon' (2/1/00)

Series 21

1. 'Lipstick And Other Problems' (2/4/00)
2. 'Under The Rug' (9/4/00)
3. 'Magic And The Morris Minor' (16/4/00)
4. 'Elegy For Fallen Wellies' (23/4/00)
5. 'Surprise At Throstlenest' (30/4/00)
6. 'Just A Small Funeral' (7/5/00)
7. 'From Here To Paternity' (14/5/00)
8. 'Some Vans Can Make You Deaf' (21/5/00)
9. 'Waggoners Roll' (28/5/00)
10. 'I Didn't Know Barry Could Play' (4/6/00)

Series 22

1. 'Getting Barry's Goat' (1/4/01)
2. 'The Art Of The Shorts Story' (8/4/01)
3. 'The Missing Bus Of Mrs Avery' (15/4/01)
4. 'Hey, Big Vendor' (22/4/01)
5. 'Enter The Hawk' (29/4/01)
6. 'Gnome And Away' (6/5/01)

7. 'A Hair Of The Blonde That Bit You' (13/5/01)
8. 'A White Sweater And A Solicitor's Letter' (20/5/01)
9. 'Why Is Barry At An Angle?' (27/5/01)
10. 'The Coming Of The Beast' (3/6/01)

SERIES 23

1. 'Potts In Pole Position' (30/12/01)
2. 'A Brief Excursion Into The Fast Lane' (6/1/02)
3. 'The Mystical Squeak Of Howard's Bicycle' (13/1/02)
4. 'Mervyn Would Be Proud' (20/1/02)
5. 'The Incredible Ordeal Of Norman Clegg' (27/1/02)
6. 'Beware Of The Hot Dog' (3/2/02)
7. 'In Search Of Childlike Joy And The Farthest Reaches Of The Lotus Position' (10/2/02)
8. 'A Chaise Longue Too Far' (17/2/02)
9. 'Exercising Father's Bicycle' (24/2/02)
10. 'Sadly, Madly, Bradley' (3/3/02)
11. 'It All Began With An Old Volvo Headlamp' (10/3/02)

SERIES 24

1. 'A Musical Passing For A Miserable Muscroft' (29/12/02)
2. 'The Lair Of The Cat Creature' (5/1/03)

xx

3. 'Ancient Eastern Wisdom – An Introduction' (12/1/03)
4. 'A Pick-Up Of The Later Ming Dynasty' (19/1/03)
5. 'The Secret Birthday Of Norman Clegg' (26/1/03)
6. 'In Which Gavin Hinchcliffe Loses The Gulf Stream' (2/2/03)
7. 'The Miraculous Curing Of Old Goff Helliwell' (9/2/03)
8. 'The Frenchies Are Coming' (23/2/03)
9. 'The Man Who Invented Yorkshire Funny Stuff' (2/3/03)
10. 'The Second Husband And The Showgirls' (9/3/03)
11. 'All Of A Florrie' (16/3/03)

SERIES 25

1. 'A Short Blast Of Fred Astaire' (21/12/03)
2. 'Jurassic – No Parking' (8/2/04)
3. 'The General's Greatest Battle' (15/2/04)
4. 'Spores' (29/2/04)
5. 'Happy Birthday, Robin Hood' (7/3/04)
6. 'Who's That With Barry And Glenda? – It's Not Barry And Glenda' (14/3/04)
7. 'An Apple A Day' (21/3/04)
8. 'Barry Becomes A Psychopathic Killer But Only Part-Time' (28/3/04)

9. 'Things To Do When Your Wife Runs Off With A Turkish Waiter' (4/4/04)

10. 'Beware Of Laughing At Nora's Hats' (11/4/04)

11. 'Yours Truly – If You're Not Careful' (18/4/04)

SERIES 26

1. 'Variations On A Theme Of The Widow Winstanley' (19/12/04)

2. 'The Swan Man Of Ilkley' (13/3/05)

3. 'Watching The Clock' (20/3/05)

4. 'Has Anyone Seen A Peruvian Wart?' (27/3/05)

5. 'Hermione (The Short Course)' (10/4/05)

6. 'Who's That Mouse In The Poetry Group?' (17/4/05)

7. 'Available For Weddings' (24/4/05)

8. 'The McDonaghs Of Jamieson Street' (1/5/05)

9. 'The Afterthoughts Of A Co-op Manager' (8/5/05)

10. 'Lot No. 8' (15/5/05)

11. 'Little Orphan Howard' (29/5/05)

CHRISTMAS SPECIAL

'Merry Entwistle And Jackson Day' (18/12/05)

SERIES 27

1. 'Follow That Bottle' (5/3/06)
2. 'How To Remove A Cousin' (12/3/06)
3. 'Has Anyone Seen Barry's Midlife Crisis?' (19/3/06)
4. 'The Genuine Outdoors Robin Hood Barbi' (26/3/06)
5. 'Barry In Danger From Reading And Aunt Jessie' (2/4/06)
6. 'Who's That Merry Man With Billy Then?' (9/4/06)
7. 'Who's That Talking To Lenny?' (16/4/06)
8. 'Oh Look, Mitzi's Found Her Mummy' (23/4/06)
9. 'Plenty Of Room In The Back' (7/5/06)

CHRISTMAS SPECIAL

'A Tale Of Two Sweaters' (28/12/06)

SERIES 28

1. 'The Second Stag Night Of Doggy Wilkinson' (15/7/07)
2. 'What Happened To The Horse?' (29/7/07)
3. 'Variations On A Theme Of Road Rage' (5/8/07)
4. 'In Which Howard Gets Double Booked' (12/8/07)
5. 'Will The Nearest Alien Please Come In' (19/8/07)

6. 'Elegy For Small Creature And Clandestine Trackbike' (26/8/07)

7. 'The Crowcroft Challenge' (2/9/07)

8. 'Must Be Good Dancer' (9/9/07)

9. 'In Which Howard Remembers Where He Left His Bicycle Pump' (16/9/07)

10. 'Sinclair And The Wormley Witches' (23/9/07)

SERIES 29

1. 'Enter The Finger' (22/6/08)

2. 'Will The Genuine Racer Please Stand Up' (29/6/08)

3. 'A Short Introduction To Cooper's Rules' (6/7/08)

4. 'Is Jeremy Quite Safe?' (13/7/08)

5. 'All That Glitters Is Not Elvis' (20/7/08)

6. 'Eva's Back In Town' (27/7/08)

7. 'In Which Romance Isn't Dead – Just Incompetent' (3/8/08)

8. 'The Mischievous Tinkle In Howard's Eyes' (10/8/08)

9. 'Of Passion And Pizza' (17/8/08)

10. 'It's Never Ten Years' (24/8/08)

11. 'Get Out Of That Then' (31/8/08)

CHRISTMAS SPECIAL

'I Was A Hitman For Primrose Dairies' (31/12/08)

SERIES 30

1. 'Some Adventures Of The Inventor Of Mother Stitch' (19/4/09)

2. 'The Mother Of All Mistakes – Or Is It?' (26/4/09)

3. 'Will Howard Cross The Atlantic Single-Handed?' (3/5/09)

4. 'Who's That Looking Sideways At Nelly?' (10/5/09)

5. 'Nobody Messes With Tony The Throat' (17/5/09)

6. 'Will Stella Find True Love With Norris Fairburn?' (24/5/09)

7. 'Will Randolph Make A Good Impression?' (31/5/09)

8. 'In Which Romance Springs A Leak' (7/6/09)

9. 'Variations On A Theme Of Father's Day' (14/6/09)

10. 'Goodnight, Sweet Ferret' (21/6/09)

INTRODUCTION

Think for a moment about all those classic sitcoms. While the premise, period, setting and style may differ, there are ingredients which are inherent in all of the examples, factors which must be in place if the programme is to rise above the norm and reach the higher echelons of the genre. Without these, the comedy – albeit watchable and likely to occasion a chuckle every now and again – will be just another run-of-the-mill product. Of course, in today's ruthless world of TV, such offerings wouldn't get a second glance, let alone a commission.

So what are some of these magical elements which are intrinsically entwined in the fabric of the best sitcoms? If we knew the answer to that we'd been overflowing with scriptwriting millionaires and not have one small-screen turkey to

Writer Roy Clarke won many plaudits for Summer Wine.

ridicule. But it's clear when you consider the likes of *Dad's Army*, *Porridge*, *Only Fools and Horses*, *Steptoe and Son*, *The Good Life*, *Fawlty Towers* et al that there are similarities – and you certainly don't need to be Einstein to spot them, either. All possess a sterling cast, for starters; performers who are adept in their craft and can bring a script to life with a single glance, a strained twitch, a puff of the cheeks.

Then there is the script itself. A proficient cast needs decent material to work with, and it's all too easy to forget the person behind the scenes, the creator whose job is to create, time after time, a high calibre script. In such a competitive arena one can only admire the ability of writers to produce an inordinate amount of crisp, rich and humorous material.

No finer example of the aforementioned qualities can be found than in Yorkshire-born Roy Clarke's scripts. A purveyor of fine dialogue and characterisation, this former teacher and policeman has afforded us the likes of *Open All Hours*, *Keeping Up Appearances* and, of course, the delectable *Last of the Summer Wine*.

If you ever wanted a seamless example of quality writing, acting and production then look no further than *Summer Wine*, the world's longest-running TV sitcom. For proof of its popularity and class, just consider how long it's been entertaining audiences: 36 years. On the surface, the show appears simply to spotlight the daily lives of, primarily, three old men ambling through their autumn years. But, as expected, there is much more to the programme, including a recurring sense of sadness, a feeling of missed opportunities and contemplating the real meaning of life, beautifully expressed through the reflective nature of the leading characters.

DID YOU KNOW?

One of *Summer Wine*'s claims to fame is that it was the first British TV comedy recorded in stereo sound.

We'll be sampling this and much more within these covers. If you want to find out how the series was conceived, discover some interesting facts about the show, learn about the writer's, performers' and producer's experiences, as well as enjoying some of the finest scenes in the long-running sitcom, which extends to over 280 episodes, then settle back and keep reading!

RICHARD WEBBER

THE STORY IN A NUTSHELL

It was the 4 January 1973 and a half-hour comedy pilot, 'Of Funerals And Fish', had just flickered on to our screens. Nora Batty was chatting with a neighbour when a small van pulled up outside. A man jumped out and disappeared into Bill 'Compo' Simonite's house next-door.

NORA: They're taking his telly again.
NEIGHBOUR: God, is it Tuesday already?

These lines provided the first breath in the life of a programme which would become a small-screen legend; it's the doyen of all sitcoms and still going strong, 36 years later. It's hard to find another sitcom which evokes so many emotions than Roy Clarke's *Last of the Summer Wine*. A sense of innocence, humour, contemplation, sadness – they're all there, embedded in scripts brought to life by a fine bunch of actors, and I'm not just referring to the main cast: even those recruited to play secondary characters or guests roles turned out well-honed performances.

But where *Summer Wine* scored extra marks is in its delicious setting. Yes, the Pennines, in the heart of Yorkshire, can be rugged, bleak and, as the performers often discovered, exceedingly chilly. But the greenery and fine curves of the rolling landscape provided a wonderful backdrop to the show.

To unearth the origins of the sitcom, we have to travel back nearly four decades to that *Comedy Playhouse* offering in the depths of winter 1973. Pioneering Duncan Wood, the then Head of Comedy at the BBC, who'd produced such shows as *Hancock's Half-Hour* and *The World of Beachcomber*, had seen Roy Clarke's comedy drama *The Misfit*, which between 1970 and 1971 ran to two series on ATV; he regarded the writer as the right man to pen a pilot script he had in mind, even though Roy had established himself, primarily, as a writer of drama.

The premise for the half-hour script centred around the daily goings-on in the lives of three elderly men – not that much happened; for them, it was about trying to fill their very long days with something to occupy their ageing minds, although they fought tooth-and-nail against the onset of old age. For a while, Roy Clarke struggled with the concept and was on the verge of declining the chance to write the pilot script; but then he found a solution to his predicament: by treating the three central characters like juveniles, with carefree attitudes and a sense of freedom akin to the years of adolescence, he created plenty of opportunities to inject humour into the script.

Everything clicked. Roy Clarke delivered a script which was shown as a pilot programme, a well-proven way of discovering which comedy ideas had the legs to become a full-blown

'WE'VE REALLY CRACKED IT THIS TIME.' (HOWARD)

series. The pilot, 'Of Funerals And Fish', was transmitted on that January evening and before long a series was commissioned. The first of six episodes, 'Short Back And Palais Glide', was screened in November 1973.

For a time, it looked as if the series would be called *The Library Mob*, despite Roy's provisional title being *Last of the Summer Wine*. Thankfully, BBC executives saw sense and opted for the writer's suggestion, which in its way symbolised the sitcom's style and format. Here, three men were reaching the twilight of their lives, despite what they may have wanted to believe, so savouring the final drops of life to the full, like you would a fine wine, were of paramount importance.

Roy Clarke's title conjures up images of rurality, too, and this aspect of the programme was an integral part of its success and longevity. For me, like millions of other fans, the characters' regular wandering on the hills, far beyond the clatter and noise of civilisation, was a crucial element – a form of escapism. It's a well-known fact that much of the filming takes place in and around Holmfirth, a small West Yorkshire town situated in the Holme Valley. Six miles south of Huddersfield, the town grew up around a corn mill and bridge in the thirteenth century, and has now been placed firmly on the tourist map, thanks to *Summer Wine*. The location was suggested by the late Barry Took, who'd filmed a half-hour instalment of a BBC documentary series close to the town; aware that Duncan Wood was shooting a Yorkshire-based comedy pilot, he recommended they take a look at Holmfirth.

The central trio of characters, beginning with Bill 'Compo' Simonite, Norman Clegg and Cyril Blamire, were written as old

friends, creating an instant bond between them and affording Roy the chance to exploit their long-held friendships for comedy purposes.

When casting the lead roles, one actor was top of the list to fill the shoes of Norman Clegg. Peter Sallis had already appeared in Roy Clarke-scripted programmes and the writer knew that upon creating Clegg, a retired lino salesman, Sallis was the man for the job. The other lead roles went to experienced thespian Michael Bates (Cyril), who'd appeared in myriad TV and big-screen roles, and equally experienced cockney actor Bill Owen (Bill).

However, the casting of Owen, whose long list of credits included the first two *Carry On* films, *Sergeant* and *Nurse*, worried Roy Clarke, who regarded Compo as the archetypal layabout. He'd only seen Owen playing roles as straight cockney, whereas Jimmy Gilbert, who produced the first series, had seen him in plenty of northern parts on stage. Roy's doubts were soon dispelled, though, when he observed Owen at the opening read-through. Now, of course, it's hard to imagine anyone other than Bill Owen playing Compo, the kind-hearted, welly-wearing scruff bag.

The personnel may have changed over the years, but *Summer Wine's* adaptability has seen it remain largely unaffected by any upheavals. Just like the *Carry On* films, where producer Peter Rogers intentionally avoided hiring star names, *Summer Wine* benefits from the same approach. Other sitcoms may have struggled if one of its leading names had departed: think of *Porridge* without Barker, *Fawlty Towers* without Cleese – well, you can't, can you? Employing well-proven and reliable character actors in the roles, intentionally or not, has enabled the programme to grow with age and cope with the changes in faces that one would expect in a programme lasting nearly four decades.

One such change was the departure of Michael Bates. When he left in 1975, he was replaced by Brian Wilde, alias Barrowclough in *Porridge*, who played Foggy Dewhurst for nine years – although he came back for a seven-year stint in the

The womenfolk enjoy their regular coffee morning at Edie's house.

9

1990s – before Michael Aldridge, as Seymour Utterthwaite, arrived for four years to make up the male trio. Then, after Wilde's second spell ended, veteran actor Frank Thornton, who'd delighted sitcom audiences with his sniffy portrayal of Captain Peacock in *Are You Being Served?*, was a last-minute replacement as Herbert Truelove.

Throughout the years, the programme has enjoyed a plethora of supporting characters. Three of the most memorable were present in the opening instalments: Nora Batty, Ivy and Sid, played by Kathy Staff, Jane Freeman and John Comer respectively. Other regulars have arrived over the years, such as Edie (Dame Thora Hird), Pearl (Juliette Kaplan), Auntie Wainwright (Jean Alexander), Glenda (Sarah Thomas), Marina (Jean Fergusson), Wally (Joe Gladwin), Wesley (Gordon Wharmby), Howard (Robert Fyfe), Barry (Mike Grady), Smiler (Stephen Lewis), Tom (Tom Owen), Alvin (Brian Murphy) and Entwistle (Burt Kwouk). All have done a sterling job under the direction of, among others, Jimmy Gilbert, Sydney Lotterby and, of course, Alan J W Bell, who has produced and directed the series for 27 years.

The series has now reached its 30th season, with Russ Abbot joining the cast as Hobbo. There is uncertainty surrounding its long-term future but regardless of how long it continues, *Summer Wine* will remain a classic sitcom and, hopefully, enjoyed by generations to come.

'HAIL SMILING MORN OR THEREABOUTS'

Blamire and Compo go into the library to look at a photo exhibition. Compo takes out one of his doorstep-sized sandwiches.

BLAMIRE: You know, if ever one of those came up in the middle of the North Sea, there'd be an international incident to decide who was entitled to stick a flag into it.

COMPO: Come on, let's go call on Clegg.

BLAMIRE: Just a moment. Just a moment. I'm studying contrast and tone. I used to exhibit myself, you know.

COMPO: You mucky old devil.

BLAMIRE: In the 14th Field Signals Regimental Camera Club, I won the Mrs. Colonel Langford O.B.E. Award for my interpretation of a soldier's farewell at F11 in 1/60th of a second. Of course, the equipment has improved since those days.

COMPO: (Sadly) Mine hasn't.

BLAMIRE: It's marvellous what you can do with a close-up lens.

COMPO: Well, hurry up and do it and let's go and get Clegg.

BLAMIRE: You've no cultural interests at all, have you?

COMPO: I've got me ferrets.

BLAMIRE: Didn't you take any advantage of the army's further education schemes?

COMPO: Well, we had this army film show once about social diseases. My mate fainted. (He approaches the display) Well it's all a lot of rhubarb this, innit? Look at this – a tatty bit of wood. Who wants to take a photograph of a photograph of a lump of wood?

BLAMIRE: It's a study in texture.

Actor Michael Bates had a long list of credits to his name when he joined Summer Wine.

COMPO: I bet that bloke had a dolly bird sitting on there.

BLAMIRE: So what?

COMPO: And he clicked his shutter and she fell off. (*He has a good chuckle*)

BLAMIRE: You've no idea, no idea at all.

COMPO: Hey up! (*looking very closely at a picture*) Hey, look at this 'ere "September Morn".

MEMORIES ...

'Duncan Wood recognised the comic element in my ITV series, *The Misfit*, and wanted me to try a sitcom. What threw me, though, was he required something for three old men – a dreadful idea, I thought. It left me cold and after playing about with it intensively for a couple of weeks, I couldn't make it work. It bored me. Then, out of desperation, I thought that if they were all footloose and free, they were in the same position as adolescents at the other end of the scale. The minute I saw them as kids, it worked.'

ROY CLARKE

'Working with John Comer [Sid] was a joy. He was a stand-up comedian and wonderful at delivering the lines. He was very popular.'

JANE FREEMAN (Ivy)

'THE GREAT BOARDING-HOUSE BATHROOM CAPER'

Foggy and Clegg are sat in the café. Ivy, in hat and coat, is at another table, gripping her handbag and looking stern. They're waiting for Compo to arrive, also Gordon with his minibus.

IVY: Are you sure you locked the back door?

SID: Thirty-three times you sent me to lock that back door. I've been up since six o'clock just locking the back blasted door.

IVY: Yes. Leave me to do all the packing.

SID: Packing? It's more like unpacking. 'You can't take *them*,' she keeps saying. 'I've no room for them. I haven't an inch of space'. Then she opens her mouth.

IVY: I heard that.

SID: And I've been hearing that (*indicating her mouth*) for nearly 30 years. Have a rest woman, you're on holiday.

One of the original cast members, Jane Freeman, plays cafe owner Ivy.

MEMORIES . . .

'Jimmy Gilbert offered me Ivy after seeing me play a dreadful landlady in *The Fishing Party*. I'll never forget recording the pilot because immediately afterwards I went on my delayed honeymoon to Greece. We had to catch a 10pm flight and with little time to prepare I went off resembling Ivy, with my normally curly hair greased down flat!

'I used to get aggressive people come up to me in the street, complaining about how I mistreated Sid; and people, usually men, would approach my poor husband, saying, "She must be hell to live with!" My late husband, director Michael Simpson, knowing the soppy me, got upset because he didn't care to be regarded as a henpecked husband.

'It's been an honour saying some of Roy Clarke's lines. In the early days, though, I thought the show was chauvinistic and questioned whether to carry on. But then Enid [Roy Clarke's wife] said to me: "You've got to remember, Ivy is me, and she's a powerful woman – she's a compliment." I didn't mind so much after that.'

JANE FREEMAN (Ivy)

'CHEERING UP GORDON'

Ivy and Sid are holidaying in Scarborough. They're sat in deckchairs on the beach. Sid is dozing in his chair making light snoring noises. Ivy is deeply involved in a women's romantic magazine. Sid snores and reality kicks in. She belts him with the magazine as she compares her husband to the hunk in her magazine.

SID: (*Startled*) What's up?

IVY: Talk to me.

SID: What.

IVY: You never talk to me not even when we, well you know …
(*in a low voice*) not even when we make love.

SID: There's not much to talk about, the rate we go at it. You still do it as if your mother's watching.

IVY: It's you, you're not thoughtful enough.

SID: Thoughtful enough? I do far more thinking about it than actually getting it.

Sid was regularly henpecked by the stern-faced Ivy.

19

IVY: That's your fault, you should … (*looking to ensure no one's in ear shot*) You should try and rouse me more.

SID: Rouse you more? (*Shouting*) You've being playing roasting hell with me all day as it is.

IVY: Will you shut up shouting, that's all you're good at, barging in with two feet. It's the same when you get that look in your eye. I always know when you feel like messing about.

SID: Messing about, that's a lovely way of putting it, isn't it? That puts it on a high spiritual plane doesn't it?

IVY: Oh, where do you put it with your smart sophisticated romantic approaches? I get a smack across the backside, a dig with your elbow, one boozy wink and that's supposed to throw my senses in a whirl.

SID: Well, it's a waste of time trying it gentle. Do you remember the last time I decided to give you a squeeze in bed?

IVY: Will you keep your voice down.

SID: Not quite, but something very similar.

20

'FLOWER POWER CUT'

Compo, Clegg and Foggy are paying their respects to their old friend Murdock, at the side of his coffin.

COMPO: *(To Clegg and Foggy)* Just one thing. When I'm dead, will you make sure that *nobody* as scruffy as me comes to my funeral?

DID YOU KNOW?

Jean Alexander, alias Hilda Ogden in *Coronation Street*, made her debut in 1988's Christmas Special, 'Crums'. Expecting her appearance to be a one-off, she returned the following year and later became a regular.

'WHOOPS'

In the café, Foggy has reassured Compo that they've got him a Christmas present.

COMPO: Well, I hope it's not useful – I hate useful presents!

'MY WIFE RAN OFF WITH A CHUFFING POLE.'
(COMPO)

SID: I only ever get useful presents. I remember one year, our lass gave me thermal underwear. You don't half know where you stand fascination-wise, when your wife buys you thermal underwear!

MEMORIES . . .

'I wanted a social battle for the conflict. With someone like Blamire and Compo, who'd be so far apart they wouldn't seek each other's company, you needed Clegg in the middle forming the anchor, bringing the two extremes together. Michael Bates was a lovely man, an ex-Ghurkha officer and right wing, whereas Bill was a socialist from way back. While making the pilot, Michael and Bill got into a political argument during the first night's dinner. Sparks were flying so Jimmy Gilbert had to whip them out to calm things down.

'It was a different series in the early days, a lot more talking heads, dialogue, and longer scenes. But you learn and some physical stuff went down well, so a lot of visual humour was introduced. It was a slow starter and wasn't until about the third season that it started picking up a better audience.'

ROY CLARKE

'IN THE SERVICE OF HUMANITY'

After hearing a minor road collision, Foggy goes rushing to the rescue.

CLEGG: I bet there's 14 dead.

COMPO: Hey-up, it were only a shunt.

CLEGG: What do we need with 14 dead, when we've got the Town Council?

Compo, Clegg and Foggy are in a pub. Foggy is wearing a red-cross tabard as Wally enters.

WALLY: I thought I might find you in here.

Peter Sallis was first choice to play Clegg.

MEMORIES …

'I was very lucky to get Clegg. When the first script arrived, I liked the comfortable feel of the idea. I hadn't worked with Bill Owen but had with Michael Bates. It's my favourite job, with a marvellous author and great directors – what more could you ask for.

'Filming had its worrying moments at times, though. One scene involved me in a canoe – and I can't swim! Before we did the scene, I was standing on the river bank. The water was moving pretty quickly and there were dark patches. When I enquired about these, I was told that's where you can't see the bottom, which made me even more nervous. When the canoe turned over, it was every man for himself. I managed to get leverage on Bill Owen's head and lift myself out of the water.'

PETER SALLIS (Clegg)

COMPO: How do, Wally.

WALLY: (*Sees Foggy's tabard*) What's this then? Have I missed something? Is it National Swiss Week?

FOGGY: Sit down, if you're stopping.

WALLY: I might, if you're not going to start yodelling. He's not going to start yodelling, is he?

FOGGY: Sit down. Nobody's going to start yodelling.

WALLY: Oh, they do, you know – they yodel. You can see it on television. They're not there two minutes before they start yodelling.

COMPO: (*Dropping the hint to Foggy*) Well, er, hang around Wally, if you've got the time, we *might* get a drink.

WALLY: (*Referring to Foggy*) Keeps it in a little barrel round his neck, does he?

'CAR AND GARTER'

Compo, Clegg and Foggy are relaxing on a hillside, as Foggy explains why he remained a bachelor.

CLEGG: How did you manage to avoid holy wedlock in that cunning manner, Foggy?

COMPO: Yeah. He were terrified.

FOGGY: It's just one of the sacrifices you have to make. No little woman waiting by the cottage door. Never the patter of tiny feet. Not being able to go browsing round Mothercare. These are just some of the snags of being a professional killer.

COMPO: Tha were a Corporal sign-writer.

CLEGG: Yes. But you should have seen him sharpen his pencil.

MEMORIES ...

'I'd worked on a drama with Peter Sallis and wanted him as Clegg. The other actors had to be old enough to be retired. We got Peter and then Jimmy Gilbert called suggesting Bill Owen as Compo. I thought it was an awful idea because I'd only seen him play cockney characters in films. But Jimmy had seen him playing northern parts in theatre and talked me into it – I'm glad he did.'

ROY CLARKE

'I inherited the programme from Sydney Lotterby and had always been a fan. It was refreshing to have a series which wasn't studio-bound. It was like winning the lottery, the nicest thing that had happened to me.'

ALAN J W BELL (Producer/Director)

'Kathy Staff and I got so fed up with Compo showing us his little matchbox that we asked how many more times we had to leap in the air with surprise. We'd screeched our way through five years so must have been accustomed to it by now. After that, he started showing it to people who hadn't seen it – whatever it was he kept inside!'

JANE FREEMAN (Ivy)

'THE ODD DOG MEN'

Sid and Ivy are in their café's kitchen, trying to open a crate.

IVY: Open it carefully.

SID: I am opening it carefully.

IVY: Well, I don't want it scratching before we even start.

SID: You've started already.

IVY: Yes, well you can't just go digging in like a lunatic, with that screwdriver.

SID: Well, pass me something sharper – like your tongue.

Compo, Clegg and Foggy are with Wally, enjoying tea and walnut cake, in Nora's kitchen. Clegg becomes uneasy on seeing Nora beckoning to him through the window.

CLEGG: *(To Foggy)* Do you ever stop to wonder if there are other beings watching us from out there?

FOGGY: I think it's highly unlikely.

CLEGG: Oh, I wish I was as sure as you are.

FOGGY: Well, it stands to reason. Well, if there was anything out there it would be doing its best to communicate with the more intelligent among us – and I've never heard a word.

CLEGG: Then you don't think that there are strange forms of life, beyond our comprehension, watching every move us humans make?

FOGGY: *(Chuckles)* No.

CLEGG: Well, in that case, I think your wife wants you, Wally.

WALLY: *(Nervously)* You think … Would you like to make sure? I should hate to go if it's not necessary.

'A BICYCLE MADE FOR THREE'

Compo, Clegg and Foggy are out walking when Compo stops to sit down.

COMPO: Hang on a minute, I've got something sharp in my welly.

FOGGY: It would have to be sharp to survive that.

Compo removes his welly to reveal a very bright pink sock.

CLEGG: Wow! It's sharp alright, is that.

FOGGY: My god! You could frighten peacocks with a sock like that.

COMPO: They was reduced.

CLEGG: Well, I'm glad to hear it. I wouldn't like to see them on full-power. What are you going to do when your battery stops?

COMPO: They're not electric.

'HE WHO WALKS WITH DANGER.' (FOGGY)

FOGGY: They are from here.

Compo peers closely into his welly.

FOGGY: *(To Clegg)* I don't know how he can do that without anaesthetic.

....

After Compo, Clegg and Foggy have been thrown out of the café, Sid reminds them how lucky they are.

SID: It's alright for you lot. She just throws you out. Me, she keeps.

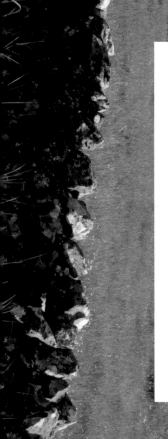

MEMORIES ...

'Although it was midsummer the light was fading fast. We were in a steep, wooded glade and this was the last shot of the day. It had been a long one and everyone was tired and looking forward to packing up and going home after the final scene was safely in the can.

'This looked increasingly unlikely in the gathering gloom. The camera crew were looking down at us from on top while I waited with the three actors – Peter Sallis, Michael Bates and Bill Owen. We were standing in a stream hoping for a change in the weather when suddenly a shaft of sunlight came through a gap in the trees, lighting the scene as if by magic.

'"Stand by, everyone," I shouted. Then, seconds later, "Action!" We were only able to shoot the one take before the sun went back in again for the day, but it was enough. It was perfect. "OK, it's a wrap!" I called.

'A voice came from the trees high above. It was Enid, standing beside her husband, the writer Roy Clarke. "I think God is looking after you, Jimmy."

'Maybe, but as things turned out, he was looking after Roy as well. We were making the pilot of a new series called *Last of the Summer Wine* that would be seen all over the world, make millions and still be running 36 years later.

'The script, then titled *The Library Mob*, had been submitted to the BBC and landed on my desk in the spring of 1972. I'd just been to Australia directing a feature film out in the Bush and had found a fantastic freedom using real locations and wide open landscapes – unrestricted by the confines of a television studio. When I read Roy's script, I was bowled over by the originality of the dialogue, the gentle quirky characters and the atmosphere of the Yorkshire countryside. I wanted to direct it in the same way as I'd done in Australia, making the scenery an important part of the series. The scripts were brilliant and if we got the casting right, I felt we were in with a very good chance.'

JIMMY GILBERT (Original director and later Head of Comedy)

'ONE OF THE LAST FEW PLACES UNEXPLORED BY MAN'

Wally is having a cup of tea in the café before going to a furniture auction. Compo, Clegg and Foggy enter.

SID: (*To Wally*) Hello. I see they're letting them out again, before they're cured.

COMPO: How-do, Wal'.

WALLY: (*Sadly*) How-do, Compo. (*To Clegg and Foggy*) How-do.

FOGGY: That's the spirit, Wally, keep looking on the bright side.

WALLY: (*Referring to Nora*) She's sending me off to an auction now.

CLEGG: Why doesn't she just divorce you, like anybody normal?

'SERENADE FOR TIGHT JEANS AND METAL DETECTOR'

To test Clegg's new metal detector, Foggy looks into his purse for a coin to bury.

COMPO: Hey-up, things must be serious if Foggy's opened his purse. I wouldn't bother with that, Foggy. We've been decimalised since tha were last in there.

DID YOU KNOW?

Jane Freeman, alias Ivy from Sid's Café, played such a tough, sharp-tongued character, constantly hectoring her hubby, she was once nearly pushed off a railway platform by a man angry at how she treated her on-screen partner.

'FROM WELLIES TO WET SUIT'

Nora opens her back-door and in bursts Compo, wearing a wet-suit and flippers.

COMPO: Ah, ha, ha! It is Nora, my little water-nymph.

NORA: Get away from me.

COMPO: Oh, Nora, come, swim with me, and between us we'll raise a pair of kippers.

NORA: Keep your fishy-fingers away from my body. Have you gone berserk?

COMPO: More than berserk, Nora. Would you like to have a look at my snorkel?

'ALL MOD CONNED'

Foggy is unhappy with Compo's choice of clothing for their holiday.

FOGGY: (*To Clegg*) We're going to have to cover him up with something.

CLEGG: Like what?

FOGGY: Well, six-feet of earth springs immediately to mind.

'THE WHITE MAN'S GRAVE'

Compo, Clegg and Foggy are in the café when Wally quietly enters and sits down.

SID: Hello, Wally, haven't you got anything to do at home?

WALLY: That's right, go on, get nasty.

SID: What did I say that's nasty?

WALLY: You said 'home'. A bloke sneaks out for a few minutes to try and forget. Next minute some clown's reminding him of home.

COMPO: Giving you hard time is she, Wal'?

WALLY: Isn't she ever?

Alan J W Bell has produced and directed the sitcom for nearly three decades.

COMPO: Well, I keep tellin' thee. Send her round to my place.

WALLY: And I keep tellin' thee: get it done up a bit and maybe she'll come.

COMPO: Hey-up, I should need a firmer promise than that, Wal', before I went to any expense.

WALLY: (*Moans*) There's always a snag.

41

SID: Eh, have you ever thought about leaving her?

WALLY: (*With frustration*) How can I? She's reduced me brain to jelly. I'm dependent on her.

SID: (*Looks towards kitchen, where Ivy is*) I know what you mean, not so much a marriage, more a life-support machine.

Who wins the prize for best hat?

'GETTING SAM HOME'

Compo, Clegg and Foggy are collecting Sam from hospital but he's not happy with his doctor's orders.

SAM: *(Reading list)* No cream cakes, no animal fats, no fornication.

CLEGG: Well, it's time you packed it in, anyway. Cream cakes at your age, disgusting!

....

Sid and Ivy are asleep in bed when they're woken by a tapping noise on the window.

IVY: *(Worried)* Listen, there's somebody at the window.

SID: Don't talk wet, we're upstairs.

Ivy turns on the lamp and they see a hand tapping on the window.

IVY: My god, there is somebody at the window. Go and see who it is.

SID: And be a male chauvinist pig? What about all this equal opportunity?

Ivy kicks Sid out of bed.

IVY: You worm, expecting your wife to go, into the clutches … it could be anybody – some lunatic desperate for a woman.

SID: Well, there you are, you see, it's for you.

Foggy, Compo and Clegg are outside their old school, reminiscing about their childhood and remembering a lost friend.

CLEGG: The thing about growing up is that you get fewer scabs on your knees, but more internal injuries.

'NORMAN CLEGG THAT WAS.' (MARINA)

COMPO: Aye, they were great days at school.

CLEGG: Oh yes, they were great days. But even then, there was no real amnesty. Do you remember the day when that little yellowhammer flew straight at the window? You picked it up.

COMPO: Aye, they've got lovely markings.

CLEGG: It had a drop of blood on its beak. Identical colour to ours. Just one drop, like a bright bead. And then there were all those brightly-plumed kids who left school, flying cheerfully and didn't get far – ran smack into World War Two.

FOGGY: That's right, look on the bright side.

COMPO: Hey, cheer up.

CLEGG: Little Tommy Naylor, lying in Africa somewhere. Blood on his beak. Identical colour to ours.

'THE LOXLEY LOZENGE'

Nora and Wally are parked-up in the motorcycle and sidecar, surrounded by beautiful countryside. Nora shouts at Wally.

NORA: Well? Talk to me, say something – anything!

WALLY: (*Thinks for a moment*) About what?

NORA: About anything, I don't care. Just talk to me. You never speak to me.

WALLY: I spoke to you yesterday. I asked you where me elastic bandage was.

NORA: That was Monday. It doesn't matter where we go, you don't talk. You just sit there. You used to like my company – once.

WALLY: Oh aye, once. But I've got it all week now.

Nora lashes out at Wally.

NORA: Don't you ever think of me as a woman? A person? Am I always just a wife?

WALLY: You've never been *just* a wife. You're about as much wife as anybody could handle. There's nobody had more wife than I have.

'BLOOD AND STOMACH PILLS.' (IVY)

NORA: You just sit there. I wonder sometimes if you'd ever miss me if I left.

WALLY: (*Cheerfully*) We could give it a try.

'THE MYSTERIOUS FEET OF NORA BATTY'

Compo, Clegg and Foggy are in the pub, trying to ask Wally a personal question.

FOGGY: We shall, of course, treat any information you might give us on this subject, in the – strictest confidence. (Shakes Wally's hand)

COMPO: Not a whisper. (Also shakes Wally's hand) You ain't got much of a grip there, Wal'.

WALLY: It's as much as I need for anything that's available to a person of my age.

CLEGG: Good grief, is it really as slack as all that?

COMPO: It is.

CLEGG: (*Shaking Wally's hand*) My god, it is, yes.

COMPO: It's like half a pound of liver.

FOGGY: Look, never mind his grip.

Some of the cast relax after filming a cafe scene in the mid-90s.

COMPO: Never mind his grip, how's he going to protect Nora with a grip like that? Suppose some bloke, who was frustrated and lonely, suddenly leapt out on our Nora?

CLEGG: My goodness, how frustrated and lonely can you get?

FOGGY: The mind boggles, doesn't it? I mean, let's be rational about this, I mean … who the heck is going to leap out on the woman, she's terrible. (*Quickly apologising*) Oh, begging your pardon, Wally.

WALLY: (*Not offended*) Point taken.

COMPO: (*Protesting*) Listen, blokes leap out on women all the time – there's me for a start!

WALLY: Well, let's face it, I'm in no condition to go punching people about.

CLEGG: Wally, you're in no condition to go screaming for help.

WALLY: (*Sadly*) It's true. If she was attacked right in front of me eyes I'd have to stand there, helpless. Helpless! She could have the bloke mauled to death before I could drag her off.

'KEEPING BRITAIN TIDY'

Compo, Clegg and Foggy have gone to Nora's to ask a favour of Wally. The men are sat in the living-room while Nora has gone to fetch Wally.

NORA: (*In the background, shouting to Wally*) Come here and see what this lot want.

WALLY: What lot?

NORA: Come and find out, and get rid of them *quick*. I don't want that lot cluttering up my house.

Wally goes into the living room and closes the door.

CLEGG: Hello, Wally.

WALLY: Ahh, human beings. We don't get many human beings. Normally it's just her lot.

FOGGY: Yes, it's just a little favour, Wally, you know. We wondered if you could give us all a lift back up the hill on your motorbike?

CLEGG: Wally, we wanted to keep it a secret from Nora, in case she invents 14 reasons for you not doing it.

WALLY: Well, it won't be a secret now. She'll be listening, she's always listening.

DID YOU KNOW?

Three of the show's popular characters — Marina, Pearl and Howard, played by Jean Fergusson, Juliette Kaplan and Robert Fyfe respectively – first appeared in a stage production of Summer Wine.

Nora storms into the room, grabs Wally and throws him out.

NORA: That's a lie, a wicked lie! (*To the men*) No, he can't give you a lift up the hill. He's far too busy.

'ENTER THE PHANTOM'

Foggy is taking Compo and Clegg to the top of a steep hill.

COMPO: (*Nearly out of breath*) Oh, oh dear, I am glad we came. Aren't you glad we came, Norm'?

CLEGG: (*Also gasping for breath*) Me? Oh, I'm just looking back nostalgically at the old days, when there used to be such a thing as oxygen.

FOGGY: Come on you men, we're nearly there.

COMPO: Nearly where? There's nowt up here.

CLEGG: Oh. Oh, don't tell me that we've come all this way and God's not in.

Peter Sallis, Brian Wilde and Bill Owen formed, arguably, the sitcom's strongest trio.

'CATCHING DIGBY'S DONKEY'

Nora and Ivy are in the café, asking Pearl about Howard's misdemeanours.

IVY: Have you any proof that he's got another woman?

PEARL: Well, not exactly proof.

IVY: Yeah, I don't mean legal proof, I mean wife proof.

PEARL: Ooh, I've got plenty of that. He won't wear the same shirt for more than two days. He's started spending hours in the bathroom.

Nora and Ivy both sigh in disgust.

PEARL: Singing!

MEMORIES ...

'I'd just returned from holiday when my agent asked me to go for an interview the following day. I said I was too busy but changed my mind on discovering it was in the evening. The part required a very aggressive lady and I remember being just that at the interview. But I was called for a second interview and recall saying, "I can't waste my time running up and down to London; you either want me or you don't." By the time I got home, a message was waiting for me, saying I'd got the part. That was Thursday and I started the following Monday. It was a mad rush because as well as learn my part, I had to find someone to run the gift shops I'd taken over since my husband's death.

'Pearl began life in the *Summer Wine* stage play in Bournemouth; I was then offered an episode on the box – just one scene. She grew from there, with Pearl, Marina and Howard forming a lovely ménage à trois which never got anywhere.

'Occasionally, people thought we'd be like our characters in real life. Once, in Wakefield, we were drinking a cuppa when this woman came over, shouting: "I'm never going to watch your show again – you tell lies. You're supposed to hate her (pointing at Jean Fergusson) yet you're having tea together!"'

JULIETTE KAPLAN (Pearl)

IVY: Is he using your talcum powder?

PEARL: I think so.

IVY: Ooh, the swine.

NORA: They always want the biggest share of everything, especially of original sin.

IVY: Yeah, I suppose God made them to go and people the planet. I just wish he'd give them a hint when to stop.

....

Compo, Clegg and Foggy are trying to catch a donkey when they stumble across Howard and Marina having an extra-marital tango.

MARINA: (*Sees Clegg*) Norman Clegg that was, who once dallied with my affections.

CLEGG: (*Retreats*) I never dallied, I never even dillied. Tell her I never dillied.

MARINA: Where's he going?

COMPO: He's got a donkey to catch.

MARINA: Damn, are the buses on strike again?

Pearl had to keep a close eye on her scheming hubby, Howard.

'UNCLE OF
THE BRIDE'

*As Howard and Pearl approach the Pegden's house to
deliver their wedding present, they see Marina leaving.*

PEARL: What's *she* doing there?

HOWARD: Pearl, love, how do I know what a certain lady, who
is almost entirely a stranger to me ...

PEARL: (*Interrupting*) Don't lie to me!

HOWARD: ... could be doing at Wesley's house?

PEARL: 'Let's call in at Wesley's place,' you said, 'and leave our
little wedding gift.'

HOWARD: I assure you Pearl, I had no idea.

Howard and Marina, the love birds, believe they've really cracked it this time.

PEARL: You've got ideas, it's always been your trouble. You've got ideas bigger than your natural capacity.

HOWARD: (*Protesting*) I've never had any complaints about my natural capacity.

PEARL: Well, you're getting one now!

Marina exchanges pleasantries, as she passes them.

60

MEMORIES ...

'I've played Howard for 24 years and it's my favourite TV role. Like Marina and Pearl, Howard was first seen in the stage show.

'It's funny what you do for television: in real life, I don't like heights but as Howard have climbed on roofs and been in a tree house; I guess you're concentrating so much on your lines and the action, you don't have time to worry about such things.

'People still ask where Marina is when I'm walking down the street – the characters are so popular. There used to be a couple who'd dress up as Howard and Marina and cycle around Yorkshire on a tandem.'

ROBERT FYFE (Howard)

MARINA: Good evening, Pearl. (*Shyly*) Howard.

HOWARD: Oh, good evening, er … er … er.

'THERE TAKIN HIS TELLY AGAIN.' (NORA)

PEARL: (*Accusingly*) Her name slipped your memory, has it? A likely story.

HOWARD: I told you, practically a stranger to me.

PEARL: You should have no problem remembering the name 'Marina'. Just think of it as a place frequented by sailors.

'THE HEAVILY REINFORCED BOTTOM'

Nora and Wally are window shopping for ladieswear.

NORA: I like that one.

WALLY: Aye.

NORA: What do you mean, 'Aye'?

WALLY: I mean, 'OK, so you like that one, great'!

NORA: Do you like it?

WALLY: Do you care?

NORA: Of course I care, I'm not going to wear something if you don't like it.

WALLY: (*Surprised*) Starting when?

NORA: Just tell me if you like it.

WALLY: Can I be honest?

NORA: Well, what's the point of me asking you if you're not going to be honest?

WALLY: Well, just remember that, and don't change your mind.

NORA: Do you like it or do you not?

WALLY: I hate it!

Nora lashes out at Wally.

NORA: You cheeky monkey, you're just being awkward.

WALLY: (*Terrified*) I like it, I like it!

NORA: I want your honest opinion, and you'd better get it right next time!

'DRIED DATES AND CODFANGLERS'

Wally has just arrived home on his motorbike when Nora comes outside to see where he's been.

NORA: Oh, there you are. What have you done with my carpet shampooer. You go off without a word. Suppose you get killed, and there's me with no carpet shampooer.

Wally can't hear because he's still wearing his helmet.

NORA: Why is he not listening to me? (*She hits him on top of the helmet*) Will you listen to me when I'm shouting at you!

WALLY: (*Removes helmet*) Good grief, woman, I thought we'd some tiles off.

MEMORIES ...

'I cast Michael Aldridge as Seymour. He had an eccentric look and was a wonderful actor with a brilliant sense of comedy. Roy had written the character as a retired headmaster of a dubious school. He had him living in a remote cottage on his own. We couldn't find anywhere and were just about to give up, thinking that Roy would have to rewrite it with the character living in the town, like everyone else, when I spotted this boarded up cottage in the distance, not more than a mile from Holmfirth.

'It was in the middle of a field owned by the Hepworth Iron Company who made pipes from clay in the land. We got permission to film, made the cottage look pretty again and even dug a duck pond. It looked serene in the programme but in reality was on the edge of the moor and the slightest wind was a gale up there.'

ALAN J W BELL (Producer/Director)

NORA: What have you done with my carpet shampooer? And don't you take another step until you tell me where me carpet shampooer is.

WALLY: Seymour said he could fix it so I let him take it to fix it.

NORA: Have you no more sense?

'GET OFF ME STEPS.' (NORA)

WALLY: He said he could fix it. He should be able to, he invents things.

NORA: Aye, what he invents most are excuses when he can't fix it. (*Wally puts his helmet on again*) And don't put your helmet back on, you can't hear me with your helmet on.

WALLY: I know. They cost a fortune, does a good helmet, but they're worth every penny.

67

'THE REALLY MASCULINE PURSE'

Clegg is contemplating the meaning of life.

CLEGG: Do you realise how fortunate it is that lips are at the front? I mean, if they were at the back, you'd never know what you were eating. On the other hand, they'd be ideally placed for kissing goodbye.

> **DID YOU KNOW?**
> The 1981 Christmas Special, *Whoops*, beat *Gone With the Wind* in the ratings.

'WHO'S FEELING EJECTED, THEN?'

Howard and Marina cautiously emerge from some woods. They're disappointed, but for different reasons.

HOWARD: I'm sorry I wasn't able to show you the caterpillar of the woodmoth.

MARINA: It came as a bit of a disappointment to me, too.

'THAT CLEARS YOUR CATARAH.' (COMPO)

HOWARD: I felt sure once we'd got among the trees, I'd be able to put me hand almost straight on to one.

MARINA: (*Sticking her chest out*) It wouldn't have come as any surprise to me!

MEMORIES ...

'The character Roy Clarke drew was outrageous but with a heart of gold. Marina evolved during the two summer seasons before I started on TV. Having a say in what she wore and how she looked, I opted for miniskirts and the brassy blonde style. Initially, though, the BBC costume department kitted me out with a low-cut red jumper and black skirt, but the following year, we went to Dorothy Perkins and bought miniskirts. A lot of her jackets, meanwhile, come from charity shops.

'I receive lots of fan mail, particularly from older men who think Marina is the bee's knees. But children, as young as nine, write saying how much they love the character.

'I'll never forget filming the episode, 'The Treasure Of The Deep'. Howard and I had to fall out a rowing boat. We were terrified, especially as we were fully-clothed. A special effects' man tipped the boat up from underneath. Robert hadn't told me he couldn't swim and was more scared than me; he ended up putting his hand on top my head, completely submerging me!

'Unfortunately, we had to shoot the scene again, once our clothes were dry and my wig – we used three different ones over the 25 years – reset.'

JEAN FERGUSSON (Marina)

HOWARD: You know what the trouble with the world is?

MARINA: What's the trouble with the world, Howard?

HOWARD: They wouldn't really believe we came out here, look-ing for the caterpillar of the woodmoth.

MARINA: (To herself, in frustration) I know just how it feels!

71

'EDIE AND THE AUTOMOBILE'

Compo comments on Nora's wrinkled stockings.

COMPO: Look at 'em – urgh, like a couple of Chinese lanterns.

....

Glenda and Barry are in their kitchen. Glenda has placed a chocolate éclair in front of Barry. Barry is in a state of shock after giving driving lessons to Edie.

GLENDA: (*Trying to be comforting*) It wasn't anything personal.

BARRY: I've never heard a motor car whimper before.

GLENDA: I just thought, you know, fresh blood. No, forget I ever said that.

MEMORIES ...

'While appearing in J B Priestley's comedy *When We Are Married* in Leatherhead, I wrote to about six light-comedy producers, one of them Alan Bell. He brought his family to see the show. He was looking for a Glenda and on the last night left a note asking me to see him – and I got the part. I'll never forget my first day's filming, though. I arrived, wearing beautiful white leather shoes and stepped out of a car into a big puddle.

'Glenda was a weak child to begin with but has grown hugely in confidence; she's showing signs of becoming like her mother, Edie, played by the late Thora Hird, who'd never allowed her to be modern. In fact, the show has always had an old-fashioned quality about it, which is one of its strengths.

'I hit it off with Mike Grady, who plays Barry, from the beginning. We've got a strong screen partnership and I love our scenes together. I'll never forget recording a breakfast scene for the episode, 'Last Post And Pigeon'. Mike was supposed to eat a boiled egg but couldn't break it open. Someone suggested using a knife but we did take after take – we were in hysterics. Eventually, he opened the egg but it whizzed across the room. But things like that happened – often the doors of Edie's Triumph Herald would stick; even the steering wheel came off once!'

SARAH THOMAS (Glenda)

BARRY: I've heard a gearbox scream, but I've never heard one whimper – unless it was me?

GLENDA: Anyway, is me mam getting any better?

Barry looks distressed again.

GLENDA: Does that mean you're not going again, Barry?

BARRY: I'm not, I'm not going again. Why did you send *me*?

GLENDA: Oh, it's not easy being torn between your father and your husband.

BARRY: It's not easy tearing between two lorries on Stackpool Street.

GLENDA: She didn't?

BARRY: I had to close me eyes after that.

GLENDA: I always think how attractive you look with your eyes closed, Barry.

BARRY: You know, I'd do anything for you, except teach your mother to drive. Honest, Brenda.

GLENDA: The name's Glenda, Barry, it's always been Glenda. You're a stranger, Barry. You won't eat your éclair and you're calling me Brenda.

Bill Owen's son, Tom, and Sarah Thomas, recruited to play Glenda.

'MERRY CHRISTMAS, FATHER CHRISTMAS'

Wesley has been summoned into the house by Edie.

EDIE: Now, wash your hands. I've run you some nice hot water – and don't splash!

WESLEY: Don't splash? Have you ever tried dabbling in water without splashing?

EDIE: Well, three people drowning wouldn't spread it about worse than you.

WESLEY: What's it all in aid of, anyway?

EDIE: All? All? I have asked you to get your hands clean, that is all. It's not major surgery. You'll be on your feet in no time.

MEMORIES ...

'Gordon Wharmby, as Wesley, was a great natural actor. When he came to see me, he'd done bits on TV, but when he read the script, he put so much character into his one line about bringing back a ladder. Impressed, I gave him another script, and although I'd already seen an actor in London for the Wesley part, I asked Gordon to read it. He made the scene very funny and real. He was a painter and decorator and had only done one-lines, but I took the chance and recruited him. He was word-perfect and got big laughs in front of the audience. Two years later, Roy brought him in as a regular character.'

ALAN J W BELL (Producer/Director)

WESLEY: I'm just in the middle of giving me engine a tune.

EDIE: Well, you can play to it later.

Gordon auditioned for a different role before landing Wesley.

'DANCING FEET'

Clegg emerges from the Co-op, where Nora and Ivy had been fending off Compo.

CLEGG: I hate being caught between Ivy and Nora, you never know which way to panic.

'TO ME, TEAM.' (HOBBO)

'THAT CERTAIN SMILE'

Seymour, Clegg and Compo are devising a plan to smuggle Clem Hemmingway's dog into his hospital ward. As the dog proves to be bad tempered, they call in at Barry and Glenda's for a sedative. Barry is coming to terms with married life.

BARRY: I can hardly believe it happened, really. I find meself stopping in front of mirrors. I look at this bloke in the mirror, and I think: 'That's you, you fool. You're married.' And do you know what's, what's really weird? I haven't got the first idea how it actually happened.

GLENDA: (*Enters room*) It happened because I have to make all the decisions for him. (*To Seymour*) We've got these travel-sick pills. They make you feel dozy.

MEMORIES ...

'I was working in the theatre when Alan Bell offered me the part. He said Brian Wilde was leaving the show and he was bringing in a new family, with Thora Hird and Michael Aldridge. He wanted me to play the son-in-law. I thought it was a one-off appearance in a feature-length episode. How wrong I was.

'The character was well written so it was obvious what was required. And I struck up a good working relationship with Sarah, who plays Glenda, and we never had a word of disagreement.

'At one point, I was working on three series at once and it was hard keeping everything going: something had to give and that was *Summer Wine*. I left the show for a while but was pleased when, later, Alan invited me back.

'I'll never forget filming the episode, "Support Your Local Skydiver", which involved a remote-controlled engine. In fact, a proper-sized engine had been placed on the chassis for the scene involving some of us opening the doors of Wesley's garage and this vehicle creeping out. But when we did the scene, it flew out, nicking me, nearly hitting others and coming close to wrecking the camera before smashing into the wall of somebody's house.'

MIKE GRADY (Barry)

SEYMOUR: Oh, they'll be fine, dear, just the job.

GLENDA: At least, they made me feel dozy. Barry went to sleep.

BARRY: What's so terrible about going to sleep?

GLENDA: We were on honeymoon!

Mike Grady (Barry) formed a strong partnership with Sarah Thomas, who played his screen wife.

'DOWNHILL RACER'

Nora and Ivy are expressing their disapproval of one of the town's women-folk.

NORA: Oh, it's a dead giveaway. Show me an expensive hair-style and I'll show you somebody who's no better than she should be.

'THE FORMER MRS TRUELOVE.' (TRULY)

IVY: No.

NORA: I always think, tidy but unattractive is the soundest base for an unblemished reputation.

IVY: (*Takes a long look at Nora*) Got it cracked then, haven't you?

'THE DAY OF THE WELSH FERRET'

Compo, Clegg and Seymour are on their way to a funeral.

COMPO: I think I'd like to be cremated.

SEYMOUR: (*Frustrated*) Oh, now he tells us, when he knows nobody's got a match.

DID YOU KNOW?

Last of the Summer Wine is the world's longest-running sitcom, having kicked off in 1973.

MEMORIES . . .

'Michael Aldridge was a nice guy. He played a different character, not as popular as Foggy, which wasn't his fault, it was mine because Seymour wasn't as obvious a character. He was eccentric enough to appeal to me, but the character's eccentricities weren't as popular as Foggy's. The same applies to Frank Thornton's character, Truly. Again, his eccentricities weren't as obvious as Foggy's, so he was never going to be as instantly popular.'

ROY CLARKE

'Over the years, Pearl has become more confident. She began as a nervous, worried little women but is increasingly outgoing and has developed a sense of humour. I love playing her. Filming in the Yorkshire countryside is lovely, too, although the show has introduced me to thermal vests and long johns – it can be freezing on those hills!'

JULIETTE KAPLAN (Pearl)

'CRUMS'

Compo, Clegg and Seymour, wearing Santa suits, are collecting for charity. They see an 'impostor' Father Christmas.

SEYMOUR: Did you see that?

CLEGG: Some *fool* dressed as Father Christmas.

SEYMOUR: It's no wonder we're not collecting any money. There's some unauthorised Father Christmas dodging about the town, beating us to it. We've got to stop him.

CLEGG: But how?

SEYMOUR: Well, we'll have to catch him.

CLEGG: I'm not running around chasing Father Christmases, dressed like Father Christmas. It'll look as if Walt Disney is in town.

MEMORIES ...

'When I wrote the pilot, Nora Batty was just the woman next door to Compo. I didn't spend any time on the character; actually, I didn't think she was a character, just a woman with a couple of lines. But she had such an impact from word one that I thought, "she's staying". Kathy Staff made her into what she became.'

ROY CLARKE

'When Michael Aldridge had to give up because his wife was unwell – he was in tears when he told me because he regarded Summer Wine as the best job he'd had – I asked Brian Wilde back; it was a logical choice because he was the most popular of the third men.

'Seymour may not have been universally liked from the beginning but grew on the fans. I think he was very funny and some of the best episodes were with him. Whereas Foggy was a leader, Seymour was the inventor who'd come up with lots of strange ideas, opening up lots of avenues for Roy. Michael Aldridge acted as a catalyst, bringing the three actors together. He even made them meet up for dinner on Sundays.'

ALAN J W BELL (Producer/Director)

'RETURN OF THE WARRIOR'

Now that Seymour has left, Compo and Clegg find themselves without any leadership so they pass the time of day in Ivy's café.

CLEGG: Suddenly, life is like first-class mail. There doesn't seem to be any urgency anymore.

'BUT I COULD BE LYING.' (TRULY)

'THE EMPIRE THAT FOGGY NEARLY BUILT'

Compo, Clegg and Foggy are at Wesley's shed, when Clegg expresses an opinion.

CLEGG: I always think it's a lot like being dead, waiting at the checkout of a supermarket.

'THE LAST SURVIVING MAURICE CHEVALIER IMPRESSION'

Howard is busy cleaning his windows, as Clegg approaches.

CLEGG: Ah, morning, Howard. Has Pearl got you started early, or have you been there since last night?

HOWARD: (*Sadly*) What's it like to be free, Cleggy?

CLEGG: Free? Sometimes I think I'm just a plaything of Foggy Dewhurst. Anyway, you don't do too badly, considering.

HOWARD: It's not easy. Pearl's got radar.

From an upstairs window, Pearl has overheard.

PEARL: (*Accusingly*) Pearl's got a what?

HOWARD: (*Thinking fast*) A radiant smile, love! I was just telling Cleggy here, how you've got a radiant smile. When you bother to use it. How come you never smile these days when you look at me?

PEARL: Smile? Because I'm too busy giggling. You look hilarious in a chilly bathroom.

She slams the window shut.

HOWARD: (*To Clegg*) You see what I mean? What do you do?

CLEGG: Well, for a start, when Pearl is around I should keep out of chilly bathrooms.

'WAS THAT NORA BATTY SINGING?'

Foggy is in the library, making an unusual request.

FOGGY: Have you anything on silent killing?

The customers in the library look around in alarm.

LIBRARIAN: (*Uneasily*) If there is anything, you'll find it under sports and pastimes.

FOGGY: Yeah. How about unarmed combat for the over-sixties? You see, I've had a look round and all I can find for the over-sixties is old-time dancing. Well, I mean, it's all very well in it's way, but if you're mugged in the street, you can hardly valletta him to death, can you?

Foggy (Brian Wilde) fancied himself as a leader of men.

'THE PHANTOM OF THE GRAVEYARD'

The three men relax in a beautiful spot. Clegg reflects.

CLEGG: You come all the way up a hill and there's this insect waiting. Now, how did it know we were coming up this hill?

> ### DID YOU KNOW?
> When Thora Hird joined the cast as Edie, she was expecting to make a one-off appearance, but her performance soon saw her become a regular.

FOGGY: You don't call these midget creatures insects.

COMPO: Here we go again. OK, what do you call insects?

CLEGG: Ronald?

FOGGY: I could tell you tales about insects. I've seen insects big enough to carry off children.

COMPO: He does talk some fanny.

CLEGG: But fluently.

FOGGY: I have seen these winged things, flying through the jungle, big as small mangles. And teeth? They could eat steel helmets.

MEMORIES …

'Brian Wilde wasn't the easiest person to work with. One of the problems was he didn't have an agent and had to do his own negotiations, always a bad move. He was also a prickly character but brilliant and never uttered a line wrong.'

ROY CLARKE

'I'd always watched *Summer Wine* and was very happy when asked to appear in the 1988 Christmas Special, 'Crums'. I always wanted to play an eccentric and this was my opportunity. It's been such a successful series because it has wonderful writing – it's so witty you could get a laugh out of every other line, if necessary.'

JEAN ALEXANDER (Auntie Wainwright)

'I received lots of letters from people saying the series has been an inspiration. Rather than just looking out the window, they now go for walks in the hills. It encourages people to do something with their lives and explore the countryside.'

ALAN J W BELL (Producer/Director)

'HAVE YOU GOT
A LIGHT MATE?'

Smiler is demonstrating Auntie Wainwright's latest money-making scheme: security-lights.

AUNTIE: People have to see what it is you're offering. They won't buy security lights if they can't see security lights.

SMILER: Supposing I get electrocuted?

AUNTIE: By the look of you, that could be beneficial.

Auntie adjusts the lights on Smiler.

AUNTIE: Yes, well, that should attract some attention.

SMILER: I feel such a fool.

Jean Alexander, who made her name playing Hilda Ogden in Coronation Street, initially joined in a one-off role.

AUNTIE: Now why should you feel a fool? Blackpool's illuminated. Blackpool doesn't feel a fool. People travel miles to see the lights. Turn round. Hmm, I wonder if there should be a red light at the rear?

SMILER: Supposing I overheat?

AUNTIE: (*Mishearing*) Not in my time, lad, you bring your own sandwiches. Well, you've got a switch. Turn yourself on.

There is a flash and a loud bang, as the lights explode.

SMILER: I think one of me bulbs has gone.

AUNTIE: (*Despairing*) That's always been my impression.

'STOP THAT BATH'

The ladies prepare to get into Edie's car, as they set off on a picnic.

GLENDA: My Barry likes a picnic. After a day in the building society he loves to be informal on the grass.

EDIE: (*Shocked*) Will you be quiet, girl! People don't want to hear things like that. You weren't brought up to be informal on the grass.

GLENDA: Oh, Mother.

EDIE: And if you get any leanings towards lolling on the grass, it's from your father's side.

'THE GLORY HOLE'

Pearl and Ivy are chatting, as usual, about Howard.

IVY: Well, what's the matter with him now?

PEARL: He's been up half the night with indigestion.

IVY: Why, what's he been eating?

PEARL: Paper.

IVY: Well, I hope you give him a bit of good gravy with it.

PEARL: It's not my paper, it's *her* paper. He thinks I don't know. He gets these notes from you-know-who.

IVY: Oh!

PEARL: Then he swallows them for security purposes. It wouldn't be so bad but it's scented notepaper.

The Yorkshire countryside played its part in the sitcom's success.

'ADOPTED BY A STRAY'

Howard is making one of his secret phone calls to Clegg. Pearl listens from the stairs until Howard notices her.

HOWARD: (*Nervously*) Hello love. I was just calling my horoscope line.

PEARL: In future, if you want to know your future, ask me.

Pearl looks at Howard.

PEARL: Why are you holding the phone down your jumper?

HOWARD: Oh, well, I always think it works better when it's warm.

PEARL: Is that why men always stand with their backsides to the fire?

'THE DEFEAT OF THE STONEWORM'

Howard has been on the phone to the council, asking about stoneworm. Pearl waits for his explanation.

PEARL: Well, what did he say? What do you use for stoneworm?

HOWARD: You apply a thin solution of vinegar and garlic.

PEARL: Garlic? I thought that was for vampires?

HOWARD: Have you checked your neck lately?

'BICYCLE BONANZA'

Compo, Clegg and Foggy are crossing the top of a waterfall when Clegg divulges information.

CLEGG: I used to think God invented beetles, but then Wesley Pegden said it was Hitler.

COMPO: Hitler invented beetles?

FOGGY: That was the Volkswagen Beetle. Hitler didn't invent creepy-crawly beetles.

CLEGG: Well, I'm glad about that. That means I can go back to liking beetles.

FOGGY: What's to like about beetles?

CLEGG: Oh, I think they're wonderful. They look like tortoises, some of them. And yet, they can fly.

COMPO: Me Auntie Meg had a tortoise.

FOGGY: She had something slow and idle and that was her husband.

When Brian Wilde left the show, Michael Aldridge was recruited as retired headmaster, Seymour, to lead the trio.

MEMORIES ...

'Bill Owen was a superb actor. Watching him, you could believe he was a Yorkshireman. But he had no Yorkshire relationship whatsoever because he was born in Acton and spoke with a London accent. He was a very friendly chap.

'Peter Sallis is a brilliant actor, too. Give him a line and he'll say it superbly, getting every bit of humour from it. He's always word-perfect and has a wicked sense of humour. I always referred to Peter as the "father" of the series. Roy Clarke gave birth to it and Peter would look after it and treasure it, making sure no one started taking it in the wrong direction. Peter cared about Roy's work.'

ALAN J W BELL (Producer/Director)

'I cast Mike Grady but it was an assistant floor manager who actually suggested him. He's marvellous, as is Sarah Thomas, who plays Glenda. She wrote to me when I was casting the character. I wanted someone who could conceivably look like Thora's daughter. She was perfect. Whenever filming is under-running, I'll ask Roy to write another scene for Barry and Glenda. Mike and Sarah will go away, have a coffee and come back word-perfect.'

ALAN J W BELL (Producer/Director)

'HOW TO CREATE A MONSTER'

Glenda and Barry have just returned home in their new car, which Barry is desperate to keep secret from Wesley.

BARRY: Are you sure you didn't tell your mother about this car?

GLENDA: I didn't tell her. I feel awful, but I didn't tell her. It were like telling lies.

BARRY: It's in a good cause. I daren't let your father near this car.

GLENDA: She wanted to know why you dropped me at the end of the street. She thinks you're up to no good. She thinks you're having an affair.

BARRY: Well, that's all right then. So long as she doesn't know about this car.

'DESTINY AND SIX BANANAS'

When a number of locals report sightings of giant apes in the woods, Foggy conscripts Compo and Clegg to assist with the capture.

FOGGY: You'll be perfectly safe. We'll be in hiding and I shall tranquilise it with one of these darts.

Foggy shows them a homemade dart, decorated with feathers.

COMPO: It's just an ordinary dart.

FOGGY: It's not an ordinary dart, it's very far from being an ordinary dart. I've prepared it with something to make the creature sleep.

COMPO: What something? Does it work?

FOGGY: Listen who's talking, does it work. No, don't worry, I've seen the natives do this in the jungle.

CLEGG: (Unsure) Yeah, they've got poisons growing in the jungle. What have you got?

FOGGY: The trained soldier learns to make do with whatever's available. You have to use whatever comes to hand.

COMPO: All right, what is it that you soak the darts in that's going to put it to sleep?

FOGGY: Well, if you must know, it's Horlicks.

'BEWARE OF THE OGLETHORPE'

The three men are reflecting on their married lives.

COMPO: It puzzles me how tha ever managed to get married in the first place.

CLEGG: Oh, it wasn't the first place, it was the third or fourth. And even then she had to ask me. Having said that, she turned out quite well, really. I was never thereafter short of a change of vest. She used to warm my underwear, every Tuesday, on a clothes-horse in front of the fire. It's amazing how close you get.

TRULY: (*Breaking the atmosphere*) The former Mrs Truelove was made of sterner stuff, until I rebelled and made her wash her own vests!

Experienced actor Frank Thornton was delighted to play retired policeman Truly.

MEMORIES ...

'Frank Thornton was my first choice as Truly. I'd been having dinner with Trevor Bannister, a neighbour of mine, who was saying how sad it was the BBC didn't repeat *Are You Being Served?* He mentioned how marvellous Frank was in it and that planted a thought in my mind. When Brian Wilde couldn't do the show because of shingles, I invited Frank in. He was overwhelmed when I asked him to play the third man. Again, it was a different character, but Frank is a work-horse and has been in comedy long enough to know how to play it. He's well loved by everybody.'

ALAN J W BELL (Producer/Director)

'The theme is gorgeous. I didn't want comedy music and Jimmy asked Ronnie Hazlehurst to write something; he came back with music which wasn't right – we wanted something sweet and nice. Ronnie went away again and within a short time was back with this wonderful theme.'

ROY CLARKE

'BEWARE THE VANILLA SLICE'

Pearl, in the knowledge that Marina had been buying vanilla slices in the café, is surprised when Howard returns home with an old lawn-mower.

HOWARD: I thought it was really time I bought something for Pearl.

PEARL: (*Suspiciously*) You bought it for me?

HOWARD: (*Pretending to be hurt*) Well, of course I did. You think I go out there and never think about you. Well, this just shows I think about you all the time.

PEARL: Did you think about we haven't got a lawn?

HOWARD: How's a bloke supposed to remember everything?

MEMORIES ...

'When we talked about the music, Roy [Clarke] was happy to leave it to me, although he didn't want anything jokey – just a good tune. A week later, Ronne Hazlehurst gave me a tape of what he'd written and I didn't like it at all. Ronnie was usually brilliant at getting the mood of a show right but the music here seemed very conventional and opposite to what Roy wanted.

"Can we have something more atmospheric?" I asked. "Something with a haunting tune – maybe a harmonica in it somewhere." Ronnie nodded and went off, apparently disappointed at my reaction. Ten minutes later, he came back and asked, "Is this the kind of thing you want?" He whistled the tune, note for note, of what has been the theme music of *Last of the Summer Wine* for 36 years. "That's not a good tune," I said, "it's a great tune." Ronnie beamed, "Well that's that fixed then."'

JIMMY GILBERT (Original Director and later Head of Comedy)

Pearl notices something on Howard's face.

PEARL: What's that on your mouth?

HOWARD: It's not lipstick!

PEARL: I can see it's not lipstick!

HOWARD: Oh, then it doesn't really matter what it is, does it?

PEARL: Wipe it off then.

Howard removes the substance with his handkerchief.

HOWARD: Oh, it's just a bit of vanilla slice.

Pearl remembers what Ivy had previously told her and sees red.

PEARL: (*Angrily*) Inside! Do you know why we haven't got a lawn? Because I'd be tempted to bury you under it!

With her trademark curlers, apron and wrinkled stockings, Nora (Kathy Staff) was one of the show's best-loved characters.

'ELEGY FOR FALLEN WELLIES'

Clegg, Truly, Nora and Ivy are sat in the hospital, waiting for news of Compo's condition.

TRULY: I wonder what put the smile on his face?

NORA: (*Rapidly covering up her black tights*) Never you mind!

CLEGG: He never used to all anything.

TRULY: (*Agreeing*) Even at school. We'd be coughing and sneezing, frog in your throat. He'd have one in his pocket.

'I AM SMILING.' (SMILER)

IVY: Ready for dropping down girls' blouses!

NORA: Took his time getting it out, though.

The girls head off for a spin, even though Thora Hird couldn't drive!

MEMORIES …

'I cast Thora Hird as Edie. My wife, Constance, suggested her. I didn't think she'd want to join us but Contance didn't agree, mentioning Thora had said it was one of her favourite programmes. She brought a huge audience with her. Constance also suggested Jean Alexander for Auntie Wainwright. She'd just come out of *Coronation Street* and agreed to do it. How lucky we were.'

ALAN J W BELL (Producer/Director)

'When Brian Wilde contracted shingles and had to drop out the series, the lines were rewritten for a retired police sergeant and I got the part. As soon as I received my first script, I knew it was good stuff – such wonderful lines.

'Deciding how to play Truly didn't take long because it was all there in the scripts; the more you can use yourself, though, the better, and as I tend to be a bit gloomy and pompous, it fitted well! It's been one of my favourite jobs and I enjoy every minute.'

FRANK THORNTON (Truly)

'SURPRISE AT THROSTLENEST'

Truly is sitting in the pub with Clegg, who is trying to pluck up courage to open Compo's letter.

CLEGG: *(Holding the letter)* This is a first. He's never written to me before.

TRULY: He's never been so far away, before.

CLEGG: *(Sadly)* Do you think he is far away?

TRULY: No, not really. The dead you care about are only next door.

CLEGG: Well, I'll drink to that.

They both raise their glasses to Compo.

TRULY: *(Impatiently)* Well, get it opened.

MEMORIES . . .

'When it came to setting the comedy, I was thinking of areas I knew, like the edges of Sheffield, but we couldn't find anything suitable. The idea of using Holmfirth came from Barry Took, who'd visited the town and thought it ideal for a TV location. I had to ask Jimmy [Gilbert] where it was, but we took a look and agreed it was just right – a remote, tight community. The location was a huge contribution to the series.'

ROY CLARKE

'Bill Owen died of cancer mid-series. If he'd died between seasons, the show would have probably finished. But, financially, we had to finish the season; I had three scripts to do, covering his death and funeral. I usually take about a fortnight for each but had just a weekend. Under immense pressure, I was able to write them. The best combination in the world is sadness and humour and I achieved that in these scripts. There was so much emotion involved, but it was important not to make the scripts too sad and to retain the bounce and funnies. It turned out to be some of the best material I've written.'

ROY CLARKE

CLEGG: I'll get round to it.

TRULY: You're making a meal of it.

CLEGG: It makes me nervous.

TRULY: What's to be nervous about?

CLEGG: He's spelt 'Clegg' with only one 'g'.

TRULY: Just be thankful you're not 'Greek'!

CLEGG: Maybe he didn't have the strength for two 'g's.

TRULY: Oh, give over, he never could spell.

CLEGG: Well, not when he was alive but, somehow, you expect dead people to spell better.

TRULY: He's only just got there. Wait til they've had him for a while.

CLEGG: I can't get used to him being dead.

TRULY: I know what you mean. Never seemed the type, did he? I mean, if he can die, nobody's safe.

'JUST A SMALL FUNERAL'

As Compo's coffin is placed in the hearse, after his funeral, his oldest friend bids him an emotional farewell.

CLEGG: We thought you'd like another wander through the hills, old son.

'DRINK YOUR COFFEE.' (EDIE)

The funeral cortège heads off through the valley, taking Compo on one last, sentimental journey.

Bill Owen played the archetypal scruff bag, Compo.

'THE MIRACULOUS CURING OF OLD GOFF HELLIWELL'

Stubborn Goff Helliwell has decided that he's going to die next Tuesday. Truly, Clegg and Billy decide to pay a visit to his bedside.

TRULY: What's this about dying next Tuesday?

GOFF: (*Adamantly*) Tuesday, that's it, finished.

DID YOU KNOW?

It was announced in 1996 that the Queen is a huge fan of the programme.

CLEGG: Aren't you supposed to be ill first, or something?

GOFF: Oh, bother that. That gets messy and inconvenient.

BILLY: Tha can't just die Goff, just like that.

GOFF: Who says, clever beggar? Just thee wait. Tuesday, it is.

His wife, Florrie, is sniffing sadly, in the background.

GOFF: Stop snivelling Florrie. I've left thee well provided for.

She leaves the room.

GOFF: Women, if they're not shouting at you, they're weeping.

CLEGG: Why Tuesday?

GOFF: She does Shepherd's Pie on Monday and I'm not missing that.

'THE CROWCROFT CHALLENGE'

Truly is watching the distant figures of Alvin and Howard through a pair of binoculars whilst Entwistle and Clegg think back to their younger days.

ENTWISTLE: Funny how life turns out. They say at school, 'What you want to be?' I say, 'Multi-millionaire'!

TRULY: Should have worn a tie.

CLEGG: Maybe they had no vacancies?

CLEGG: I committed suicide on leaving school. Well, almost. I became a lino salesman, which is as close as you can get, without a gun or a rope.

ENTWISTLE: You didn't like lino?

Actor Burt Kwouk couldn't believe it when he was asked to join the show.

CLEGG: How can you like lino? It's cold, it cracks, it smells. People used to put it in their bathrooms, which were already the coldest places on earth.

TRULY: That's why we never had fridges. The English bathroom was just as good.

MEMORIES ...

'When offered the role, I thought that of all the TV shows in the world, the one that would never offer me a job was *Summer Wine* because it's such an English show and I don't play English! But I met Alan, the director, and we got on well. I read the scripts, thought they were lovely and jokey so agreed to do a few episodes – seven years later, I'm still doing them.

'It's a lovely gentle programme. Before it's shown, we should put up a sign, saying: "This show contains no bad language, no violence and no scenes of a sexual nature." And that's what I like about it.'

BURT KWOUK (Entwistle)

'Roy Clarke is a genius, a master of words. As soon as you read the scripts you know it's quality dialogue.'

ALAN J W BELL (Producer/Director)

'I WAS A HITMAN FOR PRIMROSE DAIRIES'

Hobbo, a retired milkman who believes he used to be a secret agent, is relaxing with Alvin and Entwistle, in a beauty spot by a reservoir.

HOBBO: Should you be lying on damp grass?

ENTWISTLE: Is it damp? Risk it. Give it a whirl. Live dangerously.

'OW DO LADS.' (WESLEY)

HOBBO: It's funny you should say that, I keep getting these memory flashes. I have lived dangerously.

ENTWISTLE: Selling eggs and milk?

HOBBO: That must have been my cover.

Later on, Hobbo explains some of the pitfalls of working undercover.

HOBBO: A secret agent's no good if he's covered in Vick vapour-rub! You'd smell him for miles.

TEST YOUR KNOWLEDGE

With over 250 episodes, spanning 36 years, you have to be a mastermind to know the entire ins-and-outs of Roy Clarke's classic sitcom. But try your luck on these questions.

1. What was Compo's surname?

2. Actor Peter Sallis started his working life in what profession?

3. Foggy Dewhurst served in which section of the armed forces?

4. Which actress in the sitcom had played Miss Luke in *Crossroads*?

5. When John Comer, who played Sid, died, who arrived at the café to help Ivy?

6. What was Wesley Pegden's usual attire?

7. Frank Thornton, who played Truly, appeared as Captain Peacock in which popular sitcom?

8. Name Howard's so-called lady friend?

9. Edie, who was played by Thora Hird, had a brother in the show. What was his name?

10. Which actor played Nora Batty's henpecked husband, Wally?